21-Day Journey

Whole- Person Plant-Based Cookbook & Lifestyle Skills

Copyright © 2016 Reneé M. Beavers.

All Scriptures are taken from the Holy Bible, NEW INTERNATIONAL VERSION®. Copyright © 1973, 1978, 1984, 2011 by Biblical, Inc. All rights reserved worldwide. Used by permission. NEW INTERNATIONAL VERSION® and NIV® are registered trademarks of Biblical, Inc. Use of either trademark for the offering of goods or services requires the prior written consent of Biblical US, Inc.

This book is a work of non-fiction. Unless otherwise noted, the author and the publisher make no explicit guarantees as to the accuracy of the information contained in this book and in some cases; names of people and places have been altered to protect their privacy.

All rights reserved. No part of this book may be used or reproduced by any means, graphic, electronic, or mechanical, including photocopying, recording, taping or by any information storage retrieval system without the written permission of the author except in the case of brief quotations embodied in critical articles and reviews. Because of the dynamic nature of the Internet, any web addresses or links contained in this book may have changed since publication and may no longer be valid. The views expressed in this work are solely those of the author and do not necessarily reflect the views of the publisher, and the publisher hereby disclaims any responsibility for them.

www.reneembeavers.com.

ISBN-13: 978-0692935958

ISBN-10: 0692935959

Editor: Daphne M. Evans, The Laurel Tree Companies, LLC

www.thelaureltreecompanies.com

TABLE OF CONTENTS

- ACKNOWLEDGEMENT 5
- THE AUTHORS STORY 6
- HOW AND WHY WE DO IT! 9
- HOW AND WHY WE DO IT PART 2 11
- HOPE & TRUTH FOR YOUR JOURNEY 12
- WHAT DOES THE BIBLE SAY! 13
- WHAT DOES THE BIBLE SAY? DO THE RIGHT THING! 15
- LIVE ON PURPOSE 17
- THE MISSION OF THE MOVEMENT 19
- 21-DAY JOURNEY LIST: 21
- SHOPPING FOR YOUR NEW LIFESTYLE. 22
- REAL FOOD LESS REGRETS 23
- GUIDELINES ON THE GO! 24
- DETOXIFYING GREEN SMOOTHIE 26
- BLUEBERRY OATMEAL (HIGHLY ACTIVE) 28
- TOFU SCRAMBLE (MODERATELY ACTIVE) 30
- CHEESY GARLIC GRITS / TOFU (HIGHLY ACTIVE) 32
- MORNING MEDLEY (INACTIVE) 34
- SUPER 7 SALAD (INACTIVE) 37
- STUFFED POTATO (HIGHLY ACTIVE) 39
- TOFU WRAP (MODERATELY ACTIVE) 41
- TWO BEAN SOUP (DETOXIFYING) 43
- EGGPLANT PIZZA (HIGHLY ACTIVE) 45

- **PLANT-STRONG HOMEMADE SPAGHETTI (HIGHLY ACTIVE)** 47
- **RENEE'S DELICIOUS PLANT-STRONG BEAN BURGER (HIGHLY ACTIVE)** 50
- **CRISPY CRUNCHY TOFU NUGGETS / VEGETABLE STIR FRY (MODERATELY ACTIVE)** 53
- **BEAN ENCHILADAS (MODERATELY ACTIVE)** 55
- **OATMEAL BLUEBERRY MUFFINS (MODERATELY ACTIVE)** 58
- **KEY LIME DESSERT (INACTIVE)** 60
- **PLANT-STRONG STRAWBERRY CHEESECAKE (HIGHLY ACTIVE)** 62
- **SWEET POTATO PIE (HIGHLY ACTIVE)** 64
- **4 DRESSINGS** 66
- **OUR BOOKS** 68

ACKNOWLEDGEMENT

Thank you, God, for allowing the situation, and events, in my life that brought me to my knees. I am sure that pain and disappointment are my greatest allies. They have each made me desperate to hear and know you and your plan for my life.

I hope this book will change the life of every reader and that we would live a life that reflects the principle of making God our priority. Today, we will begin to cook meals together as a family, invite friends over and have dinner at a table together. Today, let's laugh and enjoy this incredible Journey called life together!

THE AUTHORS STORY

At a time when I should have been exploring and discovering the world around me as an 11-year-old, I was struggling with my weight. I was far too young to have started such a vicious cycle of food addiction and cereal dieting. My grandparents were organic, whole food, vegetarian advocates and as early a four-year-old I can remember them practicing and teaching the importance of eating homemade, unprocessed foods, and why pure distilled water was essential to good health. My grandmother understood the medicinal purposes of herbs, and tea and she practiced a very holistic approach to achieving and maintaining a healthy lifestyle.

Vocationally, I chose to pursue a career in cosmetology. I attended IBA College of Cosmetology, and after graduating, I passed The Michigan State Board of Cosmetology and then received my Cosmetology license within one year. My entrepreneurial journey was launched in the beauty and wellness industry. I then consumed all of my time and energy building developing and for close to 30 years.

Behind the scenes, my passion for science, nutrition and my struggle to understand and resolve my unhealthy relationships explained why food captivated and held my undivided attention. I have always been a student of my struggles and shortcomings. While must people were spending their life pursuing happiness and love, I was spending my life seeking change and solutions. I have tried every diet and exercise plan under the sun only to always come up short.

Our daughter, Aharon's diagnosis of idiopathic liver disease at the age of 11, forced me to make a decision to become a part of her solution. My quest for answers to my life-long struggle received a bit more of my attention than it had in the past. My search became more focused towards food and its relationship to illnesses. We tried many diets that claimed to provide supplements that would compensate for our nutritional deficiencies, however, we found diets can't change our life as only a lifestyle could.

In 2008, I made a decision to gain more insight by pursuing a certification in nutrition and weight management. My training provided me with the knowledge and the credentials that I needed to help myself, my family and others. Unfortunately, it only added insult to injury. Looking back, I have always felt conflicted with the concept of the food pyramid. I felt that it was out of balance and unnatural. In 2009, when my health challenge with Celiac, Arthritis, and Vitiligo further developed, instead of relying on prescription drugs, un-researched medical treatments, diets, the food pyramid, and extreme workout plans, I turned to God's age-old principles of prayer, fasting, and a Plant- Strong Lifestyle, as taught by Dr. T Collins of the China Study and Dr. Michael Greger of www.nutritionfacts.org.com.

Their books and ongoing research have provided a solid foundation to build and grow. It's a beautiful balance of biblical principles and Food Science.

Now, I totally understand why our nutritional needs are not achieved with the food pyramid. My years of experience, my study and application of the principles that I teach will provide you with the assurance needed to confirm that Regiments Lifestyle Movement is more than just a theory. Nutrition is one of the most misunderstood sciences I want to change that. I want to make plant-based nutrition crystal clear and applicable. My Certificate in plant based nutrition gives me the credentials needed. The Bible gives me the foundation and my life gives me credibility. I live a whole foods plant based lifestyle December 2018 will mark 3 years of being 100 % plant based.

Wow, what a difference in my edema and inflammation the no oil discipline made but it was a hard pill to swallow. I get it now! You can't practice a whole food plant based lifestyle and eat processed foods daily. Processed produce side effects. I will be making the necessary changes to my materials and social media platforms. I was wrong! My body and my symptoms are the evidence that a whole food plant base lifestyle is the key to a better quality of life. It is the future of personal health care. All the foods that we consume daily must be whole foods. Without exploring the cause we will never discover the cure! Food is the one area we have all over looked as the cause. Oils are not a whole food they are a food by-product a process food.

I am a whole person Plant-Based lifestyle Strategist. My primary area of focus are food addiction, serial dieting, and lifestyle diseases. I help individuals regain control their emotional, and spiritual, habits. Prayer, fasting, and a whole food plant based lifestyle are the true solutions. Helping individuals to experience true life change. In your spirit body, and mind is the mission of our movement. Please enjoy a sample reading of my latest book Freedom from Food. Join us on a personal journey of living a life with fewer regrets together.

HOW AND WHY WE DO IT!

RMB WPPB Lifestyle movement is not a diet but is instead a lifestyle for the whole person spirit, soul, and body. Our meals are designed to enhance your lifestyle by dividing them into four categories. Each of these categories is intended to help you achieve and maintain your health goals. Remember, losing weight is not the goal! Feeling better is!

Feeling better is the most valuable intangible reward without any regrets. Each of our habits builds our lifestyle. Evidence is supported by truths that are derived from the Bible and Food Science. That is the foundation of the Renee M Beavers Whole-Person Plant-Based Lifestyle Movement! A Plant -Based Lifestyle is the only lifestyle without any side effects. Fundamentally, I trust that the Bible is the only authority with results that do not cause regrets. I have always known that a strong plant lifestyle is the most beneficial lifestyle. However, this truth only lived in my mind for years.

Unfortunately, my appetite had a bigger influence on my lifestyle than the science that I was taught and the Bible that I claimed to live. Romans Chapter 14 tells us that we should practice what we know is right. When we do not practice what we know is right, we are living a lie. I believe that the Bible makes it clear that there is a correlation between our appetites and our relationship with God. Remember, Eve ate the apple, she didn't steal it or break it. Our appetites are usually the origin of our demise. Eating or not eating meat is not the real issue, practicing the principles that we know produce positive results is.

Each year, millions of Christians around the world practice fasting in January. Many call it the Daniel Fast. Most participants, who fast feel better, sleep better and some even lose weight and save money. Before February, most people run back to their lavish, disease promoting lifestyles and habits. The question is, what is causing the disconnect? What if the Daniel Fast was designed to be a way of life? What if the way to live the God created life was developed and discover by fasting? Well, I guess we will never know. Most Christians only fast 21 to 31 days out of 365 day year, if at all. Where is the Body of Proof? We are each the body of the evidence for our own life.

Revelations: 12-11 tells us that we overcome by the blood of the Lamb, the word of our testimony and by not loving our own lives unto death. This chapter of our story began last year in January, 2016.We began our annual 21 days fast with Church of the Highlands. We initially started off with a water fast transitioning to the Daniel Fast. The initial results were that my husband and I felt so much closer to Jesus and each other. We experienced mental clarity, fewer physical symptoms, less pain from arthritis and most of or inflammation was gone.

HOW AND WHY WE DO IT PART 2

With proof and evidence like this, who would not continue on this journey? Today, August 2017 we have practiced what people have called the Daniel Fast, veganism, or vegetarianism. We prefer to call it our Whole-Person Plant-Based lifestyle. Nineteen months later, our hearts, minds, skin, relationships and our quality of life is better than ever. We will never be the same. We love our new lifestyle. Church of the Highlands practices corporate fasting twice per year for clarity, direction, and to refocus. What a gift. This biblical discipline has changed our health, and lifestyle, completely forever.

We will never go back to our old life of merely existing. Today is the beginning of a new life, and a new journey and we are so grateful that we decided to practice what we believed was true! Please join us on this journey towards living a life with fewer regrets. Matthew 6:33 says to "Seek first the kingdom of God, and his righteousness and all these things will be added unto you."

I would challenge you to create a discipline that prioritizes devotional time each morning. Time to read the Bible, to pray and wait to hear God's voice daily should be paramount in our ritual. Our biggest problem with our relationship with food is that it has the wrong place in our hearts. When we put Christ first, everything else will fall into its proper place naturally. This is the principle of priority. Willpower doesn't work; the power of precedence is life changing. Make sure you start each morning with prayer, reading, thanksgiving, and adoration. Then, experience the difference prioritizing God will make in your emotional, physical, and spiritual lifestyle.

- Inactive 1000 - 5000 steps per day
- Moderately active 6000 steps per day
- Highly active 12000 and above steps per day
- Detoxifying or on a fast when you are in need of rest for your spirit soul and your digestive system

HOPE & TRUTH FOR YOUR JOURNEY

I mentioned earlier that willpower doesn't work but the power of putting God and his word first does. The Bible is full of hope and truth. Here are some verses to stand on through your journey toward living a life with fewer regrets.

- Deuteronomy 30:19:"I call heaven and earth to record this day against you, that I have set before you life and death, blessing and cursing: therefore choose life that both thou and thy seed may live:"

- Psalm 19:11-14: "Who can understand his errors? Cleanse thou me from secret faults. Keep back thy servant also from presumptuous sins; let them not have dominion over me: then shall I be upright, and I shall be innocent from the great transgression. Let the words of my mouth, and the meditation of my heart, be acceptable in thy sight, O LORD, my strength, and my redeemer."

- James 4:7: "Submit yourselves therefore to God. Resist the devil, and he will flee from you."

- 1 Peter 3:14: "But even if you should suffer for what is right, you are blessed. "Do not fear their threats; do not be frightened."

- James 4:17: "So whoever knows the right thing to do and fails to do it, for him it is sin."

- Galatians 6:9: "Let us not lose heart in doing good, for in due time we will reap if we do not grow weary."

- James 1:22: "But be doers of the word and not hearers only, deceiving yourselves."

- John 14:23: "Jesus answered, "If anyone loves Me, he will keep My word. My Father will love him, and we will come to him and make Our home with him."

WHAT DOES THE BIBLE SAY!

James 2:8:"If you really keep the royal law found in Scripture, Love your neighbor as yourself, you are doing right."

Follow the example of Jesus our Savior.

- Ephesians 5:1: "Be ye therefore followers of God, as dear children; God pours out His love on us. His love makes us want to obey Him, love Him more, and love others more."

- 1 John 4:7-8:"Dear friends, let us love one another, for love comes from God. Everyone who loves has been born of God and knows God. Whoever does not love does not know God, because God is love."

- 1 Corinthians 13:4-6:"Love is patient, love is kind, it is not envious. Love does not brag, it is not puffed up. It is not rude, it is not self-serving, it is not easily angered or resentful. It is not glad about injustice, but rejoices in the truth."

Avoid temptations to sin.

- 1 Corinthians 10:13:"No temptation has overtaken you except what is common to humanity. God is faithful, and He will not allow you to be tempted beyond what you are able, but with the temptation He will also provide a way of escape so that you are able to bear it."

- James 4:7:"Therefore, submit to God. But resist the Devil, and he will flee from you."

- John 16:7-8:"Nevertheless I tell you the truth; It is expedient for you that I go away: for if I go not away, the Comforter will not come unto you; but if I depart, I will send him unto you. And when he is come, he will reprove the world of sin, and of righteousness, and of judgment."

- Romans 14:23:"But if you have doubts about whether or not you should eat something, you are sinning if you go ahead and do it. For you are not following your convictions. If you do anything you believe is not right, you are sinning."

- Galatians 5:19-23: "Now, the effects of the corrupt nature are obvious: illicit sex, perversion, promiscuity, idolatry, drug use, hatred, rivalry, jealousy, angry outbursts, selfish ambition, conflict, factions, envy, drunkenness, wild partying, and similar things. I've told you in the past and I'm telling you again that people who do these kinds of things will not inherit God's kingdom. But the spiritual nature produces love, joy, peace, patience, kindness, goodness, faithfulness, gentleness, and self-control. There are no laws against things like that."

WHAT DOES THE BIBLE SAY? DO THE RIGHT THING!

- Psalm 34:14:"Turn away from evil and do what is right! Strive for peace and promote it!"

- Isaiah 1:17:"Learn to do what is good. Seek justice. Correct the oppressor. Defend the rights of the fatherless. Plead the widow's cause." Although we may hate sin and want to do the right thing we often fall short because of our sin nature. We all genuinely struggle with sin, but God is faithful to forgive us. We must continue to make war with sin.

- Romans 7:19:"I don't do the good I want to do. Instead, I do the evil that I don't want to do."

- Romans 7:21:"So I find this law at work: Although I want to do good, evil is right there with me."

- 1 John 1:9:"If we confess our sins, he is faithful and just and will forgive us our sins and purify us from all unrighteousness."

Don't repay people for their evil.

What does the Bible say? Do the right thing!

- Romans 12:19 Dear friends, never take revenge. Leave that to the righteous anger of God. For the Scriptures say, "I will take revenge; I will pay them back," says the LORD.

Live for the Lord and He in turn will help you to live for yourself!

- Corinthians 10:31:"Therefore, whether you eat or drink, or whatever you do, do everything for the glory of God."

- Colossians 3:17""And whatsoever ye do in word or deed, do all in the name of the Lord Jesus, giving thanks to God and the Father by him."

Put others before yourself. Do good and therefore, help others.

- Matthew 5:42:"Give to the one who begs from you, and do not refuse the one who would borrow from you."
- John 3:17:"He that hath a bountiful eye shall be blessed; for he giveth of his bread to the poor."

Do what's right and pray.

- Colossians 4:2:"Continue steadfastly in prayer, being vigilant in it with thanksgiving;"

LIVE ON PURPOSE

Each person's life has a purpose and that purpose is discovered one decision at a time on this journey called life. Unfortunately, we live in a society where most people have become followers, not thinkers. We are the total of our thoughts. Our thoughts become words, our words produce choices, our choices produce habits and our habits are the foundation of our character. However, I believe that God designed our bodies. There are a great number of metabolic diseases; we refer to them as lifestyle diseases. They are primarily a result of the habits that make up our lifestyle. What we eat, drink, think and do make up our personal lifestyles. The human body has the ability given by God to heal itself. Symptoms are an indicator of a nutritional deficiency; just like you would not ignore a light on the dash of your car, you should not ignore symptoms from your body.

The first step to beginning a Plant-Based Whole Food lifestyle is the moment when you decide to change. It's that "I decided" moment that will give you the strength to overcome the ups and down of change. The next step takes action. Detox your pantry refrigerator, freezer and your cabinets. People who have had the greatest success in transitioning into a plant-based Whole Food lifestyle are those individuals who allow their bodies to transition through a period of fasting, and fasting means to abstain-to stop. Fasting is the ultimate form of submission and personal sacrifice. Whatever controls you owns you. For something to lose its control over you, you have to stop, abstain and withdraw from that relationship.

Fasting allows your body, spirit and your mind time to remove all the residual adverse effects of the food from your body and your bloodstream. It also breaks the control food has over our life and improves our poor habits.

During your time of fasting, your appetites for the foods that you have decided to sustain from and your focus change dramatically. The staples in plant-Strong Whole Person lifestyle include fruits and vegetables (fresh and some frozen) and mostly organic nuts, seeds, and legumes. Also included are lots of herbs, and spices (fresh or dried organic) vegetable broth, organic beans and organic tomato paste, Himalayan sea salt, coconut oil, walnut or avocado oil. The best place to shop for fresh fruits and vegetables would be your local farmers market; you will have limited exposure to highly processed and artificial foods making the transition less painful. It changes your habits, and it increases your chance of long term success. Keep in mind, the RMB WPPB is not a diet- IT IS A LIFESTYLE!

THE MISSION OF THE MOVEMENT

RMB WPPB is the brainchild of Renee' M. Beavers. She is the author of **Tragedy to Majesty**. **Tragedy to Majesty** is a culmination of short and long devotionals designed to provoke and encourage personal reflection and interpersonal inventory. Knowing God is the beginning and the foundation of having an unshakable identity. When our identity is in Christ, the journey does not stop there. We begin to understand who we are and that we are loved unconditionally. The next step in our journey is getting to know ourselves intimately. You see, life is about our relationships with God, ourselves and others in that order. To add, Renee is the developer of Plant-Strong Whole-Rainbow-Rich Lifestyle Movement©. The concepts of Renee's movement will revolutionize your lifestyle like never before.

In speaking about the movement, Renee said, "It has been specially created for those people who are in desperate need of a simple system that ensures results with fewer regrets." The original vision of this movement is solely the freedom for all those individuals who are trapped in an unhealthy relationship with the food they eat. "Empowering individuals to take control of their relationship with food by leading them on a journey towards nourishing lifestyle choices that produce lasting results" is what Renee was born to do. We are one Movement with three steps which operates based on three principles, which overcome three obstacles. Cost, Time and Taste

Steps:

- Changed by fasting
- 3 Day Detox
- Freedom from Food
- 21-Day WPPB Journey
- Principles
- Priority
- Forgiveness
- Choices

- Obstacles
- Cost
- Time

When combined, all these steps guarantee a change that will bring positivity and strength to your life.

> Our team is looking forward to working with you and is ready to schedule a lifestyle session for your church, school, or salon. Contact us by phone or email for dates and availabilities. We look forward to a long relationship with you. Connect with us on social media @reneembeavers YouTube Renee M Beavers/ The Beavers BIG Journey. 404-936-1642 **reneembeavers@gmail.com**
>
> Team RMB WPPB

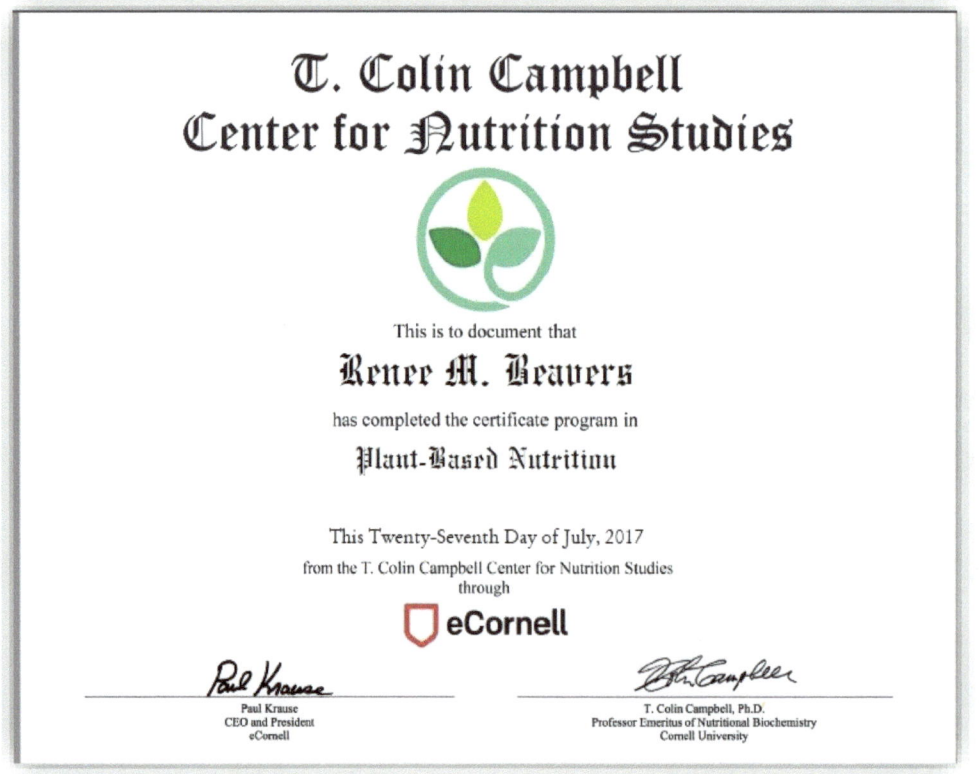

21-DAY JOURNEY LIST:

These are the essential foods to make our journey sustainable. You are welcome to purchase additional fruits and veggies. However, this list is not optional unless you have a food allergy. Each food is selected for their medicinal and high antioxidant properties. They are each essential to our journey.

*Items with stars should be eaten daily.

Watermelon*	Onion *	Clove*
Lemons *	Leeks	Cumin*
Cranberries	Beets*	Ginger *
Spinach	Walnut oil	Oregano*
Radicchio*	Avocados	Rosemary*
Broccoli	Walnuts *	Turmeric *
Cauliflower	Pecans	Apple cider vinegar*
Kale	Chia seeds	
Mushrooms *	Ground flaxseed *	
Garlic*	White tea leaves	
Hibiscus tea *		

SHOPPING FOR YOUR NEW LIFESTYLE.

We do not have a contract with the stores we are mentioning we are just providing you with the parameters and the places that we regularly shop. The best place to shop would be your local farmers market. We have found that local farmers markets have better prices on bulk real food. Our second choice would be Costco's especially for bigger families we have concluded that they are our favorite place to shop. The produce department is the only safe zone. We want to encourage Whole Plant strong foods, not processed foods. They are ok sometimes as a treat- but NOT as a lifestyle

Some of our most consumed foods are purchased at Costco. I will provide a list of those items. We also shop at Publix, Winn-Dixie, Sweet Creek Farms, and occasionally Whole Foods. Below is a list of foods and tools that every plant based home should always have other than lots of fruits, vegetables, nuts, beans, and seeds.

- Garlic press
- High-speed blender (we use the Vita Mix)
- Pressure cooker we use the Instant pot
- Rocket Chef (ideal for chopping vegetables)
- Plant Milk
- Quinoa (red or black)
- Raw local honey (Sweet Creek Farms)
- Just Mayo products (they have great plant-based mayo and salad dressing)
- Bragg's amino acids
- Green tea, Red Zinger Tea, Ginger tea.
- Montreal steak/chicken seasoning
- Old fashioned Rolled oats.
- A variety of beans: dried and canned beans.
- Sprouted tofu
- Air Fryer
- Plant cheese we prefer From Your Heart (Publix)
- Natural Nut Butters
- Vegetable Stock

REAL FOOD LESS REGRETS

I am a Whole-Food, Plant- Based, animal free, lifestyle advocate. Not eating meat does not mean that we are consuming the proper amount of whole plant-based foods required for health and wellness. Even as a vegan, vegetarian, and or meat consumer, the average individual eats far too many processed foods. RMB lifestyle Movement is more about the elements that make up your lifestyle. Daily, we must gain the power and tools to live life the way God, designed it for us in the beginning. Many of you have seen "What the Health". For some strange reason, some of you have concluded that the information was biased. Well, I stand as living proof that a whole food plant-based lifestyle is the only lifestyle proven to reverse and prevent heart disease, diabetes, and cancer to name a few.

I would love an opportunity to share the principles of our Whole-Person Plant-Strong Lifestyle Movement with your community. Our Whole-Person Plant-Strong lifestyle is built on principles that I live by each day. I am 49 years old. I have been diagnosed with celiac, arthritis, and vitiligo. However, I am not and repeat, I am NOT on any prescription drugs. I have a blood pressure of 98 over 69, my cholesterol is 172, my glucose is 100, and I weigh 135 pounds. I am healthier now than I have ever been in my life. It makes me sad and very angry to see so many of us eating ourselves to death!

I would love to teach you how to exchange your traditional recipes for their healthier, more affordable, nutritious, plant-based varieties. It's time to stop existing in denial. It's time to live the abundant God designed LIFE we were all created for with hope in freedom with Liberty! Please join us on this journey of living a life with fewer regrets!

GUIDELINES ON THE GO!

Eating on the go guidelines: Remember we don't have control over that which is being produced in grocery stores or restaurants. However, we do have control over what we choose to buy and consume. These little changes will make a difference. If the missing elements in our lifestyle are vitamins and minerals why do we focus on protein? That one nutrient is not going to help to achieve the goal of total Health and Wellness.

One of the goals of our movement is to consume colorful whole, unprocessed foods as close to the way God created them as possible. Eat smaller portions, slowly and around a table with others. When you're out and on-the-go, remember the rainbow is always the most important requirement. The essential color is green. Make sure you consume dark rich colors: red, orange, yellow and purple; the more vibrant the colors, the more nutritious the option. Before you order or eat anything ask yourself these 5 questions:

1. Is this real food; can I recognize and pronounce the ingredients?
2. If I left it out on my counter would it spoil?
3. Will this add to or take away from the good bacteria in your digestive tract? (Remember your digestive system feeds on healthy bacteria like fiber.)
4. Will this choice lead to reward or regret?
5. Is this going to make me feel good and energized, or bad and lethargic?

Mindset shift:

Free your mind of your old way of thinking, and your life will follow.

Call to Action:

Begin to consume your meals on smaller plates; this is an excellent way to control portions.

Exchange: Old habits: Large processed food options, eating extremely fast alone in a car.

New habit: Smaller whole plant derived meals eaten slowly, with others at a table.

Please join us on this journey of living a life with fewer regrets Providing hope, freedom, and liberty, for individuals trapped in unhealthy relationships, with the foods they eat and the relationships that are eating them.

DETOXIFYING GREEN SMOOTHIE

Ingredients

- 1 lemon
- 5 cups of spinach
- 2 Dates
- 1 Banana
- 1/2 cup of mango
- 1/2 cup raspberries or strawberries
- 2 Tablespoons of ground flaxseed
- 4 oz. of Plant-Strong milk
- 1 oz. of green tea
- 1/2 cup of ice

Directions

Add dates pitted, plus raspberries and green tea and blend until smooth. This is the recommended base for all smoothies; you may add any variety of fruits and vegetables to your base. The more ice used the thicker the smoothie. Please remember to drink your smoothie slow and with a straw. Please rinse your mouth with water after you finish your smoothie. This will protect your teeth from the acid in your smoothies.

Bon Appetite!

Minutes to Prepare: 20

Number of Servings: 4

Cost Per Serving: $2.50

Smoothie Rainbow:

- Green: Spinach / Avocado/ Kiwi
- Dark Green/ Kale/ Apple/Cucumber
- Orange: Papaya/ Mango
- Red: Raspberry/Strawberry/ Dragon Fruit
- Purple: Blueberry Grapes/Blackberry
- Yellow: Banana/Pineapple
- Pink: Watermelon/Strawberry

Notes:

BLUEBERRY OATMEAL (HIGHLY ACTIVE)

Ingredients

- 1/2 Cup of old-fashioned rolled oats.
- 1/2 Cup blueberries.
- 1/2 Cup plant strong milk.
- 1/2 Cup water
- 1 Teaspoon cinnamon
- 1 tbsp. sugar

Directions

Minutes to Cook: 45

Number of Servings: 1

Cost Per Serving $1.75

Combine milk, water, and old-fashioned rolled oats. Cook for about 5 minutes then add blueberries and cook for another 3 minutes add sugar and cinnamon. Bon appetite!

Notes:

TOFU SCRAMBLE (MODERATELY ACTIVE)

Ingredients

- 1/2 cup of tofu
- 1/2 cup bell peppers, onions and mushrooms.
- 1 clove of garlic
- 1/2 cup of Super 7 salad
- 3 tablespoons l
- 1/2 tsp. Montreal chicken and steak seasoning.

Directions

Minutes to Cook: 20

Number of Servings: 1

Cost Per Serving: $2.00

Add grape seed oil and garlic onions, bell peppers, tofu and spices and herbs into preheated skillet. Sauté until brown. When golden brown color is achieved add super seven salad. Bon appetite.

Notes:

CHEESY GARLIC GRITS / TOFU (HIGHLY ACTIVE)

Ingredients

- 1/2 cup of plant strong milk (soy or almond plain)
- 1 slice smoked Gouda cheese (Follow Your Heart)
- 1/2 cup of water
- 3 tablespoons of grits
- 1/4 teaspoon of Montreal steak seasoning Himalayan sea salt.
- 3 tablespoons veggie broth 1 clove of fresh garlic

Directions

Minutes to Cook: 20

Number of Servings: 1

Cost Per Serving: $1.50

Combined water and milk into a pot with 1/4 teaspoon of Himalayan sea salt and add 3 tablespoons of grits. Boil until a creamy consistency is achieved. Add plant strong smoked Gouda, grape seed oil and garlic. Bon appetite!

Notes:

MORNING MEDLEY (INACTIVE)

Ingredients

- 2 cups fresh cut watermelon
- 1 cup grapes
- 1/2 a cup of pineapple or papaya
- 1/2 cup Berry
- 1/2 melon
- 1 teaspoon cinnamon
- 1/2 cup pumpkin seeds, almond, or Walnut.
- 1 cup of plant strong yogurt plain

Directions

Minutes to Cook: 20

Number of Servings: 1

Cost Per Serving: $2.70

Visit our YouTube channel. Renee M Beavers for instructions on how to cut watermelon

Combined all fruit in a bowl and add with cinnamon and yogurt.

Bon Appetite!

Notes:

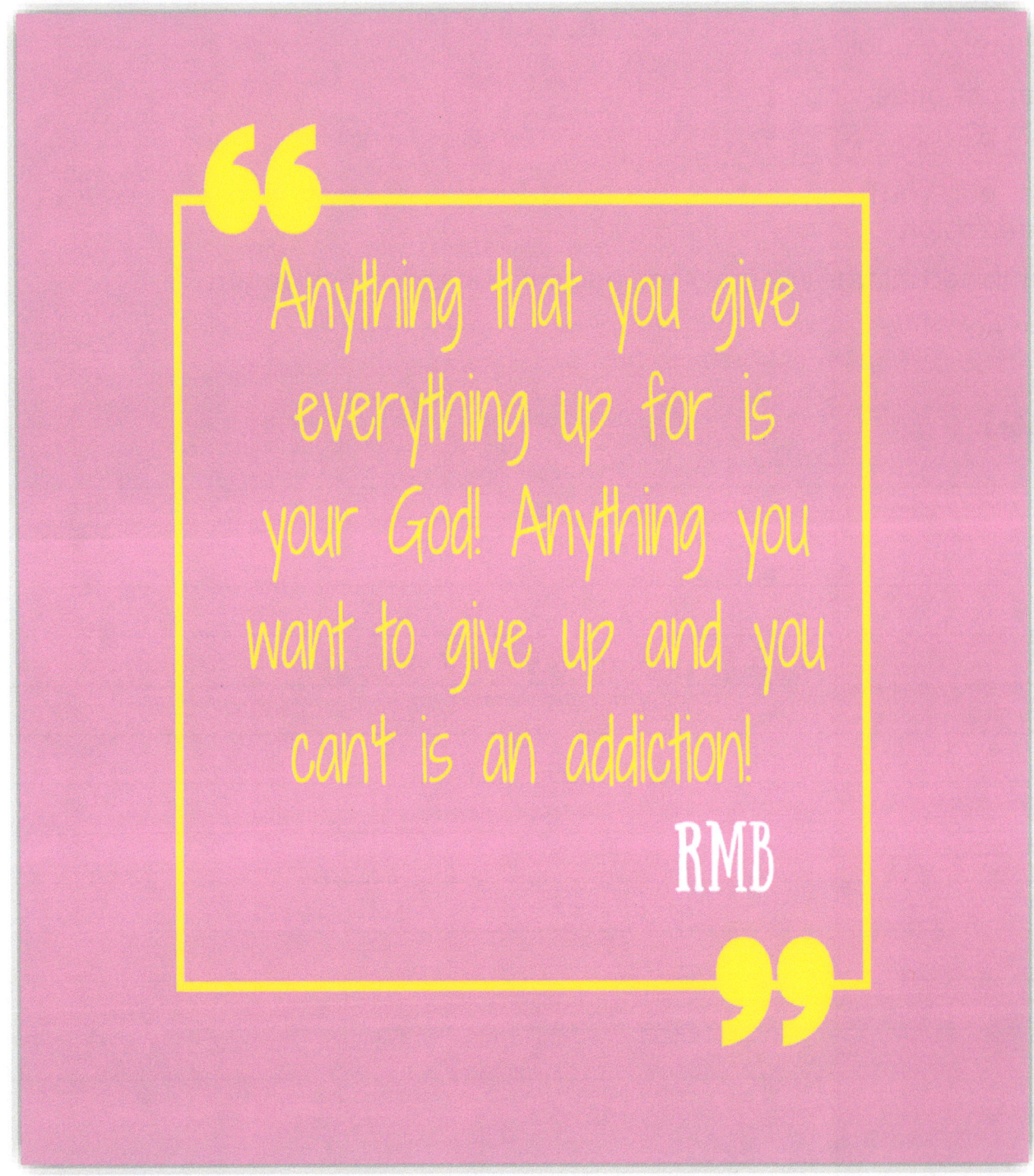

SUPER 7 SALAD (INACTIVE)

Ingredients
- 1 cup Spinach
- 1 cup Super-7 salad
- 1/2 cup of olives
- 1/2 cup tomatoes
- 1/2 cup bell peppers
- 1/2 cup sliced apples
- 1/2 cup walnuts pumpkin seeds, raisins.

Directions

Minutes to Cook: 15

Number of Servings: 1

Cost Per Serving: $1.75

2 Tablespoon poppy seed dressing or plants strong mayonnaise.

Bon Appetite!

Notes:

STUFFED POTATO (HIGHLY ACTIVE)

Ingredients
- 1 Potato
- 1 cup broccoli, kale or spinach.
- 1/2 cup onions, bell peppers, mushrooms.
- 3 Tablespoons of Plant-Strong cheese.
- 1 Tablespoon nutritional yeast
- 1 teaspoon Montreal steak and chicken seasoning.

Directions

Minutes to Cook: 20

Number of Servings: 4

Cost Per Serving: $1.75

Wash, then score potato with fork, wrap in foil and bake for 45 minutes. Sauté bell peppers, onions and mushrooms add seasonings. Stuff sautéed vegetables into potato and bake for 10 minutes with plant-based cheese.

Bon Appetite

Notes:

TOFU WRAP (MODERATELY ACTIVE)

Ingredients

- 1/2 Cup tofu
- 1 Cup Super-7 salad
- 1 Tablespoons Nut Butter
- 1 Gluten free tortillas
- 1/4 tablespoon plant strong mayonnaise.
- 1/2 Teaspoon Montreal Steak & chicken seasoning.

Directions

Minutes to Cook: 20

Number of Servings: 6

Cost Per Serving $2.50

Add pre-made crispy tofu

Pan brown Gluten free tortilla. Add plant strong mayonnaise and Super 7 salad. Bon Appetite

Notes:

TWO BEAN SOUP (DETOXIFYING)

Ingredients
- 1 Bag of lentils
- 1 Bag of split peas
- 1 Vidalia onion
- 1 Green pepper
- 3 Cloves of fresh garlic
- 1 Box of vegetable broth
- 3 Tablespoon Montreal Steak and chicken seasoning
- 2 Tablespoons of coriander and cumin

Directions

Minutes to Cook: 20

Number of Servings: 6

Cost Per Serving: $1.50

Wash split pea and lentils in a colander. Sauté vegetables until light golden brown. Add beans and vegetables in large pot with full content of vegetable broth, 16 ounces of water, spices, and herbs on medium heat for 60 minutes until smooth creamy consistency is achieved.

Bon Appétit!

Notes:

EGGPLANT PIZZA (HIGHLY ACTIVE)

Ingredients

- 1 eggplant - 3 inches in diameter, peeled and cut into 4 half-inch thick slices
- 1 cup Super-7 salad (Costco)
- 1/2 teaspoon salt, 1/2 teaspoon garlic, 1/2 teaspoon Italian seasoning
- 1/8 teaspoon ground black pepper
- 1/4 cup organic pasta sauce
- 1/4 lb. smoked Gouda cheese

Directions

Minutes to Cook: 12

Number of Servings: 4:

Cost Per Serving: $2.50

Preheat the oven or toaster oven to 425 degrees F. Season with the salt and pepper. Arrange on a baking sheet and bake until browned and almost tender- about 6 to 8 minutes, turning once. Spread 1 tablespoon of pasta sauce on each eggplant slice. Top with super 7 salad and plant cheese. Bake until the cheese melts, 3 to 5 minutes. Serve hot.

Bon Appétit

Notes:

PLANT-STRONG HOMEMADE SPAGHETTI (HIGHLY ACTIVE)

Ingredients:

- 4 or 5 vine ripe roma tomatoes
- 3 large peeled squash
- 1 pack of gluten free pasta
- 1 large clove of garlic
- 3 fresh basil leaves
- 1 Tablespoon Walnut or grapeseed oil
- 1/4 teaspoon of oregano
- 1/4 teaspoon of Rosemary
- 1/2 of a red or green pepper
- 1/2 of 1 onion
- 5 large mushrooms sliced very thin
- 1/4 Teaspoon of Montreal steak seasoning
- 3 Tablespoons of ground flaxseed

Minutes to Cook: 20: Number of Servings: 6

Cost Per Serving: $2.10

Direction.

In a blender, combine tomatoes and all ingredients excluding the mushrooms and squash until a smooth consistency is achieved. If you are preparing the "raw" 21-Day Journey spaghetti dish, your sauce will be complete. For the cooked version, take the contents of the blender and put it in a saucepan sautéing on low heat until a deep red color and reduced water is achieved.. You are also welcome to add additional sautéed vegetables like eggplant; bell peppers; onions; mushrooms and of course, spinach. With your spiralizer, take your peeled squash and spiralizer until each squash is a beautiful plate of squash pasta. For the cooked version, boil gluten free pasta in a saucepan. It cooks a lot quicker when you add pasta to hot water drain add delicious homemade spaghetti sauce.

Bon Appetite!

Notes:

RENEE'S DELICIOUS PLANT-STRONG BEAN BURGER (HIGHLY ACTIVE)

Ingredients

- 1 can drained black beans mashed
- 1 cup of precooked eggplant
- 1 cup of portabella mushrooms and Vidalia onions sautéed
- 2 cloves of raw garlic
- 1/2 cup of almond flour
- 1/2 cup of gluten free oats
- 1/4 cup of ground flaxseed
- 1 tsp Montreal steak seasoning
- 1 teaspoon of Himalayan sea salt

Directions

Minutes to Cook: 20

Number of Servings: 4

Cost Per serving: $2.60

Sauté all of your vegetables until they're brown and caramelized and allow them to cool. Combine seasoning, mashed refried beans and all of the vegetables as well as the oil and all dry ingredients. Place them into circular patties on a piece of parchment paper. Allowed your patties to chill in the refrigerator for about 20 minutes before cooking them in a very warm skillet lightly oil skillet. A good tip is to pre-wrap some of the extra patties for later and places them in

the freezer. This recipe makes about 10 thin patties or 5 thick patties. Add your favorite toppings and use your favorite bread toast.

The bread also makes it more like a restaurant burger.

Bon Appetite!

Notes:

THE WEIGHT OF WAITING

IT RESTS ON YOUR CHEST LIKE 200 POUNDS OF STEEL AND JUST BEFORE YOUR LAST BREATH, FROM DEEP WITHIN, YOU GAIN THE STRENGTH TO BEGIN TO SLOWLY RELEASE THE PRESSURE OF ITS WEIGHT BY PRESSING IT UP. IN THE PROCESS OF PRESSING, YOUR FOCUS SHIFTS FROM THE WEIGHT TO FINDING THE STRENGTH TO FREE YOURSELF. AS A RESULT OF PRESSING, YOU'RE NOW STRONG, AND NOW YOU SEE THE BENEFITS OF WAITING.

IF WAITING WERE A PERSON SHE WOULD BE CONSIDERED RUDE, BARKING OUT HER DEMANDS AND DIRECTIONS WITHOUT EVER TAKING INTO CONSIDERATION THE EFFECT HER PROCESSES WOULD HAVE ON HER VICTIMS, FORCING THEM TO COME AND GO, START AND THEN STOP, NEVER SAYING PLEASE OR THANK YOU. SHE ONLY HAS ONE GOAL IN MIND: TO TEACH WHAT ONLY SHE CAN, HOW TO WAIT .WAITING IS SUCH AN ESSENTIAL PART OF THE HUMAN EXPERIENCE; HOWEVER, IT'S EXTREMELY OVERLOOKED.

WE ARE SO FOCUSED ON LIVING LIFE THAT WE IGNORE THE FACT THAT WE SPEND A GREAT DEAL OF OUR LIFE WAITING. YOU AND I ARE TAUGHT MANY OTHER LESSONS IN OUR LIFETIME. UNFORTUNATELY, WE ARE NEVER FORMALLY TAUGHT TO WAIT. UNLIKE SO MANY OF OUR OTHER LIFE LESSONS, WAITING DOES NOT NEED OUR PERMISSION TO HAVE HER WAY IN OUR LIFE. SHE WILL NOT REQUEST OR NEED AN INVITATION. WAITING IS SOMETHING THAT WE HAVE NO CONTROL OVER, AND IT'S ALMOST UNCONSCIOUS. WE WAIT ON GOD, WE WAIT ON PEOPLE, AND WE WAIT ON SITUATIONS AND CIRCUMSTANCES, WE ARE CONTINUOUSLY WAITING.

WAITING IS SOMETHING THAT WE PRACTICE EACH DAY OF OUR LIVES. WAITING IS WHERE OUR REAL CHARACTER IS DEVELOPED AND REVEALED. WE KNOW THAT WE DON'T HAVE CONTROL OVER WHETHER WE WAIT OR HOW LONG WE MUST WAIT. UNLIKE SO MANY OTHER LIFE LESSONS, NO ONE IS EXEMPT FROM WAITING. IT'S NONNEGOTIABLE. WHAT DO WE HAVE CONTROL OF? WE CAN WAIT WITH OUR ARMS FOLDED HAVING A TEMPER TANTRUM. WE CAN WAIT WITH A NEGATIVE, ANGRY ATTITUDE.

WE CAN ALSO WAIT MURMURING AND COMPLAINING, PLAYING THE HELPLESS VICTIM. THESE, ARE LEGITIMATE OPTIONS MEANWHILE NONE OF THESE WILL MAKE OUR WAITING SHORTER. THE NATURE OF WAITING MEANS THAT WE CAN'T RUSH HER OR CONTROL HER. I WOULD SAY THE ONLY BENEFICIAL WAY TO INTERACT WITH WAITING IS TO CHOOSE TO YIELD AND BE OPEN. WAIT PATIENTLY AND USE THE TIME WISELY BY USING THE TIME AS PERSONAL REFLECTION. WAITING IS OUR GREATEST GIFT AND OUR ALLY TO A LIFE WITH FEWER REGRETS. THE CHOICE IS YOURS, AND YOU CAN CONTINUE TO FIGHT AND ARGUE WITH HER. HER RESPONSE WILL CONSISTENTLY REMAIN THE SAME... SO WAIT.

READ COMPLETE CHAPTER 1 TIMOTHY 2:1-3 KING JAMES VERSION (KJV 2 I EXHORT THEREFORE, THAT, FIRST OF ALL, SUPPLICATIONS, PRAYERS, INTERCESSIONS, AND GIVING OF THANKS, BE MADE FOR ALL MEN; 2 FOR KINGS, AND FOR ALL THAT ARE IN AUTHORITY; THAT WE MAY LEAD A QUIET AND PEACEABLE LIFE IN ALL GODLINESS AND HONESTY. 3 FOR THIS IS GOOD AND ACCEPTABLE IN THE SIGHT OF GOD OUR SAVIOR;

www.reneembeavers.com

CRISPY CRUNCHY TOFU NUGGETS / VEGETABLE STIR FRY (MODERATELY ACTIVE)

Ingredients

- 1 pack of extra firm tofu
- 1/2 Cup of gluten free all-purpose flour
- 1/2 Teaspoon of Montreal steak, chicken seasoning, garlic powder.
- 1/2 Cup of Super 7 salad
- 1/2 Cup Mushrooms
- 2 Cloves of fresh garlic
- 1/2 of Vidalia onion
- 1/2 of red bell pepper
- 1/2 cup purple cabbage

Directions

Minutes to Cook: 40

Number of Servings: 4

Cost Per Serving: $1.75

Drain tofu on paper towel. Slice into square chunks blot with paper towel and then season with spices and herbs. Place into a clear zip lock bag of gluten free flour and shake. Then place in refrigerator. Slice onions, bell peppers and mushrooms and leave on cutting board. Place individual squares of tofu in Air Fryer. Cook until golden brown placing the crispy crunchy tofu to the side. In a sauce pan add onions, bell peppers, mushrooms and sauté to light golden brown. Then, add cabbage. Sauté until soft and then add Super 7 salad last. For about 1 minute, place on a bed of vegetables and add tofu squares. (Save extra tofu in plastic bag for use throughout the week. Bon Appetite!

Notes:

BEAN ENCHILADAS (MODERATELY ACTIVE)

Ingredients
- 1 small onion, chopped
- 1 small green pepper, chopped
- 1/2 cup sliced fresh mushrooms
- 1 garlic clove, minced
- 1/2 Teaspoon of Montreal steak, chicken seasoning
- 1 can (15 ounces) black beans, rinsed and drained
- 1 can (15 ounces) kidney beans, rinsed and drained
- 1 can (4 ounces) chopped green chilies
- 2 tablespoons reduced-sodium taco seasoning 1 teaspoon dried cilantro flakes
- 6 Corn tortillas (6 inches), warmed
- 1/2 cup enchilada sauce
- 3/4 cup shredded Plant –Strong Cheese

Directions

Minutes to Cook: 20

Number of Servings: 6

Cost Per Serving: $1.75

In a large skillet, sauté the onion, green pepper and mushrooms in oil until crisp-tender. Add garlic and cook 1 minute longer. Add the beans, corn, chilies, taco seasoning and cilantro; cook for 2-3 minutes or until heated through. Spoon 1/2 cup bean mixture down the center of each tortilla. Roll up and place seam side down in a 13-in. x 9-in. baking dish. Top with enchilada sauce and cheese. Bake uncovered at 350° for 25-30 minutes or until heated through. Yield: 6 enchiladas. Bon Appetite!

Notes:

OATMEAL BLUEBERRY MUFFINS (MODERATELY ACTIVE)

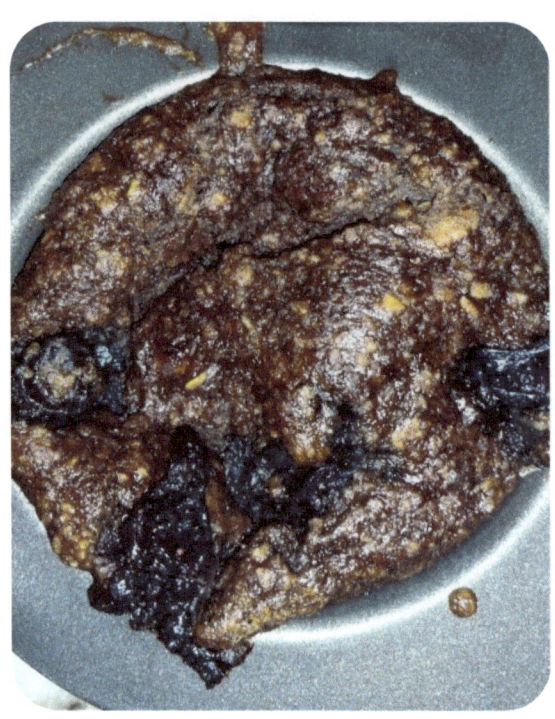

Ingredients

- 1 Cup + 3 tablespoons of
- 1 Cup of old fashioned oatmeal
- 1 Cup Gluten-free or all-purpose
- 1 tablespoon of gluten free baking powder
- 1 pinch of salt
- 3/4 Cup of dates and molasses combine 2 totals 3/4 cup
- 1/3 cup plus 2 teaspoons of a cup of almond milk
- 3 tablespoons of flax mixed with 8 tablespoons of water
- 1 small bananas mashed
- Half of a cup of fresh blueberries
- 1 teaspoon (of each) cinnamon, ground cloves, and allspice.
- Bake on 350 for 30 minutes

Directions

Minutes to Cook: 20

Number of Servings: 12

Spray 12 large or 18 regular muffin pans. Line pans you can also use a few 4" loaf pans. Grind 1 cup old fashioned rolled oats in the food processor or clean coffee grinder until finer than cornmeal. Stir all the dry ingredients together very well in a bowl. Beat wet ingredients together in a separate bowl with a whisk or fork. Make a well in the center of the oat mix and stir in the egg mix, stirring to blend. Spoon batter into greased muffin pans. Bake at 400 F oven for 20 minutes. Turn out onto wire rack to cool. Fabulous hot served.

Bon Appetite!

Notes:

_____
_____
_____
_____
_____
_____
_____
_____
_____
_____
_____

KEY LIME DESSERT (INACTIVE)

Ingredients

- 2 Avocados
- 1 Lime juice and zest
- 1 Tablespoon of nut butter
- 2 teaspoons raw honey
- 1/2 Cup of pitted dates
- 1/2 cup pecans

Directions

Minutes to Cook: 20

Number of Servings: 6

Cost per serving: $1.25

Chop dates and pecans. Mash fresh avocados and remove zest, then squeeze lime. Combined and then add raw honey. Press pecan and date mixture on the bottom of the pan and then add avocado and key lime filling. Refrigerate for 2 hours.

Bon appetite!

Notes:

PLANT-STRONG STRAWBERRY CHEESECAKE (HIGHLY ACTIVE)

Ingredients

Crust:
- 1/2 cup raw almonds
- 8-10 Medrol dates

Cheesecake:
- 2 cups raw cashews (soaked overnight)
- 1 1/2 cups fresh strawberries
- 1/2 cup maple syrup
- 1/3 cup Nut Butter (measure after melting)
- Juice from 1 lemon
- 1/2 tsp sea salt

Directions

Minutes to Cook: 20

Cost per serving: $1.10

Number of Servings: 6 Soak the cashews for at least 4 hours (or overnight).Add the pecans, dates, coconut, and sea salt to a food processor and process or chop until a slightly sticky, crumbly dough is achieved. Press dough into the bottom of 22 mini cupcake sections using the back of a spoon and your fingertips. This makes the crust for the cheesecakes. Place them in the freezer while you make the strawberry cheesecake filling .Clean and dry the food processor. Drain the cashews and add those plus the strawberries, maple syrup, coconut oil, and lemon juice to the food processor and turn on for a couple minutes until a thick, creamy filling form. Take the muffin tin out of the freezer and fill each with the strawberry cream filling. Sprinkle with a few chocolate chips and freeze for at least an hour. Allow to thaw for 15 minutes before serving. Bon Appetite

Notes:

SWEET POTATO PIE (HIGHLY ACTIVE)

Ingredients

- Three large baked sweet potatoes
- 1/4 cup of raw sugar
- 1/4 cup ground golden flax
- 1/4 cup Nut Butter
- 1/4 cup organic maple syrup
- 1/4 cup of almond coffee creamer
- 1 Tablespoon rum extract
- 1 tablespoon, cinnamon, nutmeg, allspice

Directions:

Minutes to Cook: 60

Number of Servings: 6

Cost per serving $1.00

Combine the following in a bowl: peeled bake sweet potatoes, grape seed oil, maple syrup, rum extract and almond coffee creamer. Blend until smooth. (Don't forget to remove all strings from yams.) Add all dry ingredients including the preferably gold ground flaxseed in a bowl and blend until smooth. Score pie crust with a fork then add sweet potato filling in pie crust and bake for 45 minutes at 350 degrees allow to cool.

Bon Appetite!

Notes:

4 DRESSINGS

SAVORY AVOCADO:

Ingredients:
- 1 Avocado
- Juice of 1 lime
- 2 Tablespoon vegan mayo
- 2 Tablespoons Braggs apple cider vinegar
- Minutes to Cook: 10
- Number of Servings: 4

CREAMY GARLIC:

Ingredients:
- 2 Tablespoons Braggs apple cider vinegar
- 2 Tablespoons of Nut Butter
- 4 Tablespoons Hampton Creek Just Mayo
- 1 Clove of Raw Garlic
- 1/4 teaspoon of oregano.

BALSAMIC TALIAN:

Ingredients:
- 2 Tablespoons Braggs apple cider vinegar
- 2 Tablespoons of Nut Butter
- 1/4 teaspoon Italian seasoning,
- 1 raw garlic clove,
- Juice of 1 lemon.
- 1/4 cup Balsamic vinegar or raspberry vinegar.

TOMATO ISLAND:

Ingredients
- 3 Tablespoons of Just Mayo
- 1 Tomato raw blended
- 3 Tablespoons of relish
- 2 Tablespoons of apple cider vinegar

Directions for All:

Blend on low in blender until smooth store in Mason jar in refrigerator. Bon Appetite!

OUR BOOKS

- Tragedy To Majesty - Alone With God And Your Thoughts: Lifestyle Devotional
- RMB WPPB 21-Day Journey: Plant -Strong Whole -Person Cookbook
- Freedom from Food: 6 week Small Group Curriculum
- Coming Soon
- The Empty Marriage : Working Towards Oneness
- Unstoppable Warrior Woman :Collaboration
- B3 Business Beyond Beauty: Unforgettable Salon Experiences

www.ingramcontent.com/pod-product-compliance
Lightning Source LLC
Chambersburg PA
CBHW060809090426
42736CB00003B/207